Rocky Mountain National Park

John Hamilton

VISIT US AT
WWW.ABDOPUB.COM

Published by ABDO Publishing Company, 8000 West 78th Street, Suite 310, Edina, MN 55439.

Printed in the United States.

Editor: Sue Hamilton
Graphic Design: John Hamilton
All photos and illustrations by the author, except National Park Service, p. 26 (bighorn sheep), and
Enos Mills, p 12.

Library of Congress Cataloging-in-Publication Data

Hamilton, John, 1959-
  Rocky Mountain National Park / John Hamilton.
      p. cm. -- (National parks)
  Includes index.
  ISBN 978-1-60453-094-0
  1. Rocky Mountain National Park (Colo.)--Juvenile literature. I. Title.

F782.R59H36 2009
978.8'69--dc22
                          2008011892

Contents

An elk gazes out over the Gore Range, near Trail Ridge Road.

Top of the World

Colorado's Rocky Mountain National Park lives up to its name, literally. More than one-third of the park is above the treeline, higher than 11,500 feet (3,505 m). It is the highest national park in the United States, home to 72 mountain peaks towering over 12,000 feet (3,658 m). The tallest, Longs Peak, soars 14,259 feet (4,346 m), kissing the sky. Dozens of alpine lakes, sparkling like blue jewels on the landscape, rest upon giant slabs of granite. Some of the mountains contain rocks that are nearly two billion years old, as ancient as those found in the bottom of Arizona's Grand Canyon.

Thanks to Trail Ridge Road, a winding highway that straddles the Continental Divide, park visitors can experience landscape seldom seen by humans. In the thin air of the alpine tundra—the land above the trees—specialized animals and delicate plants fight to survive howling winds and freezing temperatures. At first glance, the landscape seems barren, but pikas, yellow-bellied marmots, and white-tailed ptarmigan thrive here.

Although Rocky Mountain is best known for its alpine tundra, there are three other distinct ecosystems in the park. The subalpine ecosystem rests between 9,000 and 11,400 feet (2,743 and 3,475m) in elevation. Spruce and fir trees that survive in this cold, wind-swept landscape are twisted and gnarled. During the short summer season, huckleberry and juniper shrubs thrive, dotted by colorful wildflowers. Martens and long-tailed weasels prey on rabbits and pikas. Boreal owls hunt mice at night.

Farther down in elevation is the montane ecosystem, between approximately 5,600 and 9,500 feet (1,707 and 2,896 m). Thick forests of long-needled ponderosa pine—some 400 years old—mix with aspen, lodgepole pine, and Douglas fir. There are also grassy hillsides and beautiful mountain meadows. Deer and elk graze on grass and shrubs that grow between the widely spaced trees. As the pine trees age, their bark becomes cinnamon-red, releasing a pleasing scent into the mountain air. In June and July, wildflowers splash the hills with color. In autumn, quaking aspen leaves turn golden-yellow, shimmering in the cool breeze.

Rocky Mountain is famous for its bighorn sheep and elk. In September and October, large herds of elk gather in the lower elevations. The haunting bugling of bull elk echo through the woods, signaling the fall rut, or breeding season.

Other animals that live in Rocky Mountain's montane ecosystem include black bear, bobcats, coyote, skunk, moose, and Abert's squirrel. The rasping screeches of red-tailed hawks can be heard overhead. Hiding in the dense underbrush are mice, chipmunks, and other small rodents.

Glacier-carved valleys support a rich riparian (wetland) ecosystem. Rocky Mountain contains more than 150 lakes and 450 miles (724 km) of streams. Vegetation is thick around riparian areas, which also include marshes, wet meadows, and beaver ponds. Inhabiting these cold waters are a variety of fish and amphibians, including greenback cutthroat trout. Rare boreal toads can sometimes be found near shore, although their numbers are dwindling.

Chipmunks and other small animals are commonly spotted along the hiking trails of Rocky Mountain National Park.

A small pond at the end of Old Fall River Road (above). The tundra ecosystem here is too cold to support trees. Farther down the mountain, a grove of aspen thrive (below).

Glacial Landscape

Rocky Mountain National Park occupies about 265,770 acres (107,553 ha) of land in the Front Range of north-central Colorado. Just a couple hours north of Denver by car, traveling to the park is an easy way to see alpine landscape that is normally too high up or too far north to visit.

The soaring peaks and majestic valleys of Rocky Mountain were created by fire and ice. Hundreds of millions of years ago, sediments accumulated on the floor of an ancient sea, hardening and crystallizing into metamorphic rock. Volcanic activity added thick layers of magma, which turned into granite.

Starting about 70 million years ago—during the age of the dinosaurs—violent shifts in the earth's crust drove these layers of rock upward, forming mountains. This process continued for millions of years. Erosion—the unstoppable forces of wind, rain, and ice—ate away at the mountains, forming the craggy peaks we see today. During the past two million years, glaciers ebbed and flowed over the landscape. These rivers of ice, some more than 500 feet (152 m) thick, carved deep, U-shaped valleys, called cirques. Boulders and rock debris left over when the glaciers retreated formed moraines, or ridges, that allowed mountain lakes to form.

Small glaciers still exist in the park, including Andrews Glacier, Taylor Glacier, and Mills Glacier. These permanent snowpacks exist high in the mountains, where temperatures rarely climb above freezing.

Snowpack lingers well into the summer months in the park's highest elevations.

Dream Lake rests in Tyndall Gorge, with Hallett Peak in the background.

"The mountain trail is rich with the spice of life.

History in the Park

Enos Mills

Glaciers shaped the valleys and peaks of Rocky Mountain National Park. During the time these rivers of ice scoured the landscape, humans seldom ventured into the area.

Starting about 10,000 years ago, as the glaciers retreated, nomads began venturing into the mountains, hunting woolly mammoths along ancient game trails. Although early Native Americans never made the area their permanent home, some were able to live off the land during the short summers. The most dominant tribe to settle here were the Utes, or Mountain People. The Cheyenne and Arapaho also occasionally traveled into the mountains from their homes on the plains.

By the late 1700s, European-Americans began exploring the area. Fur trappers sought valuable beaver pelts. In 1859, the Pikes Peak gold rush brought large numbers of miners to the area. Homesteaders began appearing in the 1860s.

Harsh winters meant that ranching never really took hold in the area. Tourism, however, began to boom when people discovered the grand beauty to be found in the mountains just north of bustling Denver. By 1900, conservationists, including the tireless Enos Mills, urged the government to make the area federal land, setting it aside for future generations.

On January 26, 1915, President Woodrow Wilson signed a law making Rocky Mountain a national park. Enos Mills, with hope in his heart, wrote, "In years to come when I am asleep beneath the pines, thousands of families will find rest and hope in this park."

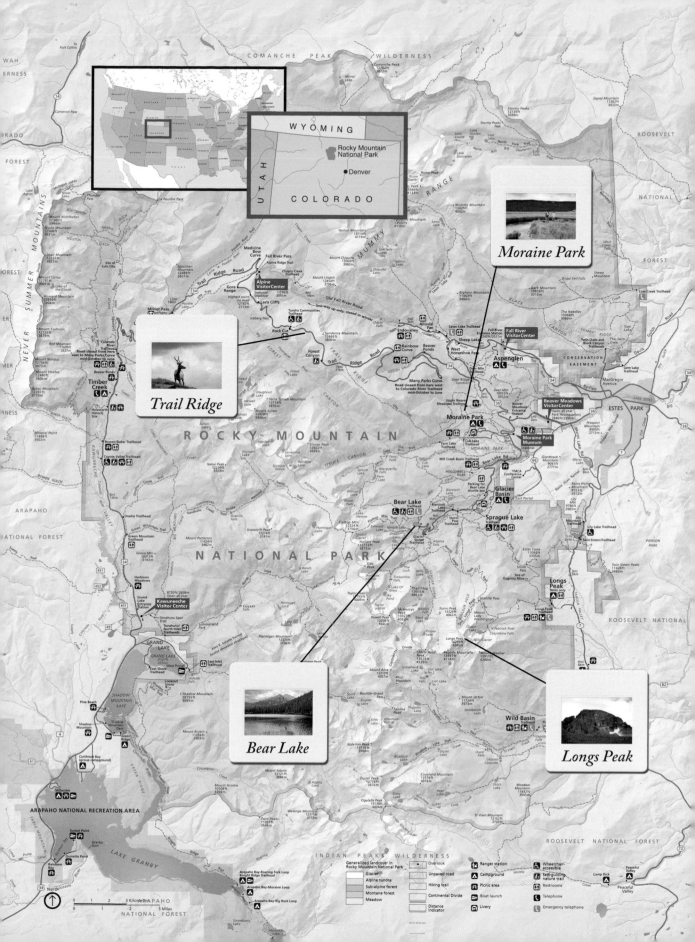

Trail Ridge Road

When people visit Rocky Mountain, they don't just visit a park; they go to the top of the world. Trail Ridge Road is by far the biggest attraction. Long considered one of the most scenic drives in America, it is the nation's highest paved highway. One stretch follows a mountain ridge that climbs to a height of 12,183 feet (3,713 m). At altitudes like these, the landscape becomes alien. Alpine tundra is a treeless, windy, often bitterly cold place, where only specialized plants and animals dare live. This ecosystem is found only on the highest mountains, or in the far reaches of the Arctic. And yet, in Rocky Mountain, it is only a couple hours away by car, easily visited after a picnic lunch or a shopping trip in the bustling tourist town of nearby Estes Park.

Other famous national parks of the West, such as Yellowstone, Glacier, and the Grand Canyon, were connected by railroads during their early history. Not so with Rocky Mountain. Cars have always been the way most people visited the park. During the Great Depression of the 1930s, the National Park Service put unemployed people to work building Trail Ridge Road. The new paved highway connected the east part of the park with the west, straddling the rugged mountains of the Continental Divide, which runs north and south through Rocky Mountain.

The twisting, winding, always-breathtaking road transports visitors from forests and meadows up to the heights of treeless alpine tundra, and then back down again. From Estes Park in the east to Grand Lake in the west, the road stretches for 48 miles (77 km) across the park, rising almost 4,000 feet (1,219 m) in altitude. It's a fascinating experience, traveling from dense forests to tundra in so short a time. It's like driving to northern Canada or Siberia in only an hour.

Trail Ridge Road provides 48 miles (77 km) of mountain scenery

Trail Ridge Road is open from mid-May until October, when it closes because of heavy snows. Starting just west of the town of Estes Park, the road begins its climb at Deer Ridge Junction. It approximately traces the path of a 10,000-year-old game trail that prehistoric hunters once used. The road steadily climbs upward, through forests of pine. At Many Parks Curve, an overlook gives stunning views of the mountain valleys that spread out below you. (In Rocky Mountain, a "park" is a mountain meadow.)

Farther up the mountain, the road enters the tundra. At Rock Cut, you can take a stroll through this wind-swept landscape. Take care not to trample alpine forget-me-nots and other delicate flowers and mosses. With a growing season of only 40 days, damaged plants can take decades to recover. The tundra is full of life and color, if you look close enough. Pikas, marmots, and ptarmigan use ingenious camouflage to hide from hungry predators. Larger animals wander into the upper elevations in the summer months, including herds of elk and bighorn sheep.

At the Alpine Visitor Center, you can explore a nature center, talk to park rangers, or simply stand in front of the floor-to-ceiling windows and gawk at the mountain scenery. A short walking path leads from the visitor center to the top of a ridge that gives panoramic views of the surrounding mountains. The thin air here can leave you literally breathless. People accustomed to lower elevations sometimes are short of breath, so take your time and enjoy the scenery. Always be on the lookout for quick-changing weather; thunderstorms can sneak up and drench unwary visitors in a matter of minutes.

The Alpine Visitor Center, near the top of Trail Ridge Road. The logs on the roof protect the building from the heavy snows the park receives in winter.

Sunset on alpine tundra along Trail Ridge Road (above), high above the treeline. Inside the Alpine Visitor Center (below), tourists take shelter from an afternoon thunderstorm.

After crossing the Continental Divide at Milner Pass, travelers can stop at Farview Curve for a spectacular view of the Never Summer Mountains bordering the northwestern part of the park. Visitors are few in this rugged network of peaks, but hardy backpackers and hikers are rewarded by stunning views of snow-covered granite peaks and sparkling alpine lakes. The mountains rise so high that many are named after cloud types, such as Mount Stratus and Mount Cumulus. In the late 1800s, prospectors combed this area, searching for gold and silver. The abandoned shacks of mining towns, such as Lulu City, can still be seen.

Continuing on, Trail Ridge Road descends rapidly into the scenic Kawuneeche Valley, which lies along the western edge of the park. The forests here are thicker, and the rains more frequent, than the eastern side of Rocky Mountain. Twice as much moisture falls on this side of the Continental Divide. When clouds rise up to cross the mountain barrier, they drop much of their water, which feeds the lush vegetation of the valley. Moose are often seen in this part of the park. The mighty Colorado River, which stretches halfway across the country before it empties in the Gulf of California, has its humble beginnings here.

Kids play on a fence near the Continental Divide.

The Clark's Nutcracker likes to eat seeds from large pine trees.

*Wildflowers cling to a boulder resting in Sprague Lake (above), along Bear Lake Road.
Hallett Peak (below) towers over the Bear Lake trail area. Tyndall Glacier is to the right.*

An elk (above) forages for food in the alpine tundra along Trail Ridge Road. The Big Thompson River (below) cascades through a boulder field near Moraine Park.

Bear Lake Road

One of the most popular parts of Rocky Mountain National Park is Bear Lake Road. This 10-mile (16-km) stretch starts just beyond the park's Beaver Meadows Entrance Station. It's a pleasant ride that skirts valleys and hillsides, leading through stands of aspen and lodgepole pine. As the winding road heads south toward Bear Lake, it crosses cascading rivers, edges past crystal blue lakes, and borders mountain meadows filled with elk and other montane ecosystem wildlife. Because the road is often overcrowded during tourist season, the Park Service runs shuttle busses that whisk visitors to major stops along the way.

Moraine Park is a large, glacier-carved valley that was once a ranch, then a major tourist resort complete with a golf course. Today the area has returned to its wilderness roots. Elk freely roam the open spaces, and trout swim in Big Thompson River, which runs through the middle of Moraine Park. Horse rides are available through Hi Country Stables, the only stables located in the park. The Moraine Park Museum, which features natural history exhibits and a nature trail, is located near the homestead of Abner Sprague, a pioneer and resort owner who helped popularize the park.

Sprague Lake (named after Abner) has a wheelchair-accessible trail that meanders through woods and hugs the shoreline. Early mornings, which are less crowded, feature splendid views of thick forests and distant mountains. Fishing is a popular activity.

At the end of the road is Bear Lake, which can be explored by walking an easy half-mile (.8-km) trail that circles the shore. Brochures at the trailhead point out interesting scenery and facts about forest ecology along the way.

A chipmunk (above) rests on a boulder on the edge of Bear Lake. A pair of anglers (below) fish for trout in Big Thompson River, which runs through the middle of Moraine Park.

Hiking

Longs Peak

There are more than 350 miles (563 km) of hiking trails in Rocky Mountain National Park. On warm summer days, some of the most popular paths can be quite crowded. In other areas, walk just a few minutes off the trailhead and it seems as if you have the park to yourself. Destinations are as varied as your imagination: interpretive nature trails circling subalpine lakes, hikes to tumbling waterfalls, or all-day treks to the highest mountain peaks.

Starting at the Bear Lake trailhead, well-used paths meander through the woods. A short walk up the valley is Nymph Lake, a beautiful mountain jewel studded with yellow and green water lilies. Farther up the trail, about one mile (1.6 km) total, is Dream Lake, with breathtaking views of Hallett Peak and Flattop Mountain looming in the distance. A short path to the east takes you to Alberta Falls. Here Glacier Creek thunders down a series of cascades, making it one of the park's most popular hikes.

Challenges await in the park's less-visited areas. A hike in Wild Basin, in the south part of Rocky Mountain, might include a trip to Bluebird Lake and Ouzel Falls. A recovering part of the forest, once charred black from a major fire in 1978, now blooms with wildflowers. In the remote Mummy Range to the north, and the Never Summer Mountains in the west, experienced backpackers enjoy a wealth of overnight camping possibilities.

Longs Peak, the tallest mountain in the park at 14,259 feet (4,346 m), has long attracted the adventurous. No technical climbing experience is needed during the short summer season, but wise visitors plan ahead for a challenging hike. Most people begin their trip before dawn in order to be off the mountain by afternoon, when fast-moving thunderstorms and dangerous lightning often arrive.

A family of day-hikers (above) packs food, water, and fishing gear for a trek to Dream Lake along a trail in Tyndall Gorge, southwest of the Bear Lake trailhead. Many park trails lead to streams and waterfalls, such as this cascade below Alberta Falls (below).

Horseshoe Park

Bighorn sheep

Horseshoe Park is a mountain meadow located just west of the town of Estes Park, on the northeastern side of Rocky Mountain. It is a popular area for hiking, biking, wildlife viewing, and fishing. The mountains of the Mummy Range, just to the north, are a favorite destination of backpackers and horse riders.

The horseshoe-shaped valley was once covered by a glacier 500 feet (152 m) thick. For hundreds of years, the river of ice inched forward, scouring the landscape. When the glacier finally melted, it left behind the distinctive U-shaped valley. Today, the wet meadows are home to moose, black bear, deer, beaver, and muskrat. A natural salt lick near Sheep Lakes attracts the park's famous herds of bighorn sheep. During the autumn breeding season, competing males fight for the attention of females. The sound of their horns crashing together can sometimes be heard up to one mile (1.6 km) away.

Old Fall River Road is a one-way gravel road that begins in Horseshoe Park. Completed in 1921, it is the first road to cross the Continental Divide inside the park. Although it was replaced in the 1930s by the more modern Trail Ridge Road, Old Fall River Road can still be driven all the way to the top of the valley, ending at the Alpine Visitor Center. It's a winding, leisurely drive, with plenty of wildlife viewing and mountain scenery. After tunneling through a thick conifer forest, the road eventually climbs above the treeline, revealing alpine tundra for the last few miles of the route.

The one-way, gravel Old Fall River Road (above) ends at the park's Alpine Visitor Center, high in the alpine tundra. The road begins in Horseshoe Park (below), a mountain valley that was once covered by glacial ice 500 feet (152 m) thick. Today it is a prime wildlife viewing area.

Future Challenges

Even though Rocky Mountain National Park is only about one-eighth as big as Wyoming's Yellowstone National Park, it gets about the same number of tourists. About 3.3 million people visit the park each year. Most of them come during the peak summer season. This overcrowding often strains the park's roads and facilities. The increase in housing and commercial development from the town of Estes Park, which borders Rocky Mountain's east side, only adds to the pressure. Budget cuts have made responding to the problem difficult. The National Park Service has helped ease overcrowding somewhat by creating a system of shuttle busses, especially along popular Bear Lake Road.

One natural problem that is affecting Rocky Mountain, and many pine forests of western North America, is the spread of wood-eating beetles. About 17 species of these insects burrow through the bark of conifers to lay their eggs. When hatched, the hungry larvae devour the inner bark of the trees. The stressed trees turn reddish or gray, and then eventually die. During the last decade, warm winters and low rainfall amounts, possibly because of global warming, add to the problem. To fight the pine beetles, the Forest Service uses insecticides on individual trees in high-use areas.

Ranger Jack Dailey answers questions and helps control crowds at the Bear Lake information station.

Many pine trees of mountainous western North America suffer from wood-eating beetle infestation (above). Warmer average temperatures in recent decades have made the problem worse. Shuttle busses (below) help lessen overcrowding in Rocky Mountain National Park.

Glossary

ALPINE

In high mountains, alpine is the vegetation zone above the treeline, where it is too cold for trees to grow.

CONTINENTAL DIVIDE

A ridge of the Rocky Mountains in North America. Water flowing east of the Divide eventually goes to the Atlantic Ocean. Water flowing west goes to the Pacific Ocean.

ECOSYSTEM

A biological community of animals, plants, and bacteria, all of whom live together in the same physical or chemical environment.

FEDERAL LANDS

Much of America's land, especially in the western part of the country, is maintained by the United States federal government. These are public lands owned by all U.S. citizens. There are many kinds of federal lands. National parks, like Rocky Mountain National Park, are federal lands that are set aside so that they can be preserved. Other federal lands, such as national forests or national grasslands, are used in many different ways, including logging, ranching, and mining. Much of the land surrounding Rocky Mountain National Park is maintained by the government, including several national forests and wildlife refuges.

FOREST SERVICE

The United States Department of Agriculture (USDA) Forest Service was started in 1905 to manage public lands in national forests and grasslands. The Forest Service today oversees an area of 191 million acres (77.3 million hectares), which is an amount of land about the same size as Texas. In addition to protecting and managing America's public lands, the Forest Service also conducts forestry research and helps many state government and private forestry programs.

GLACIER

A glacier is often called a river of ice. It is made of thick sheets of ice and snow. Glaciers slowly move downhill, scouring and smoothing the landscape.

SUBALPINE

A growth zone in the mountains that exists just below the treeline.

TUNDRA

Tundra is normally thought of as the vast, almost treeless plains of the Arctic regions. Some mountains, like those in Rocky Mountain National Park, are so high and cold that tundra conditions exist on their upper elevations.

WETLAND

A wetland, sometimes called riparian, is an area of land that usually has standing water for most of the year, like swamps or marshes. Many wetlands have been set aside as preserves for wildlife. Many kinds of birds and animals depend on this habitat for nesting, food, and shelter.

Longs Peak, framed by two aspen trees growing at Upper Beaver Meadows near Moraine Park.

Index